Decodable Little Books

20 Reproducible Little Books for Short Vowel Sounds

by Christine E. McCormick

Illustrated by Jill Dubin

Good Year Books

Parsippany, New Jersey

Acknowledgment
The author thanks Laura Feuerborn for her illustrations of the books used during the try-out phase.

Good Year Books
are available for most basic curriculum subjects plus many enrichment areas. For more Good Year Books, contact your local bookseller or educational dealer. For a complete catalog with information about other Good Year Books, please write:

Good Year Books
An imprint of Pearson Learning
299 Jefferson Road, P.O. Box 480
Parsippany, NJ 07054-0480
www.pearsonlearning.com
1-800-321-3106

Book Design: April Okano
Design Manager: M. Jane Heelan
Managing Editor: Suzanne Beason
Executive Editor: Judith Adams
Cover Design: Elaine Lopez

ISBN 0-673-59241-3

2 3 4 5 6 7 8 9 – ML – 06 05 04 03 02 01

Decodable Little Books

20 Reproducible Little Books for Short Vowel Sounds

Preface

Decodable Little Books consists of twenty reproducible, easy-to-decode books for children learning to blend individual letter sounds into words. In the style of Good Year Books' successful *Little Books, Little Books from A to Z,* and *Little Books 1,2,3, Decodable Little Books* presents a few words of text on each page with supporting illustrations. The first 10 books use primarily a single short vowel sound (two books for each vowel). The second 10 books use several short vowels in the words of the texts, and gradually add a few more short words per page.

All of the books help develop fluency in reading short decodable words. While many other early reading books mix sight words and decodable words, *Decodable Little Books* supports the strategy of systematically blending each letter's sound into the word. The only sight words in the texts are "the" and "a."

Table of Contents

13. Dot and Sam *(short 'a,' 'i,' and 'o' sounds)*

14. Sam and Dot *(short 'a,' 'i,' 'o,' and 'e' sounds)*

15. Peg and Zip *(short 'a,' 'i,' 'o,' and 'e' sounds)*

16. Peg and Gus *(short 'a,' 'o,' 'e,' and 'u' sounds)*

17. Dot and Peg *(short 'a,' 'i,' 'o,' 'e,' and 'u' sounds)*

18. Gus and Zip *(short 'a,' 'i,' 'o,' 'e,' and 'u' sounds)*

19. Gus, Sam, and Peg *(short 'a,' 'i,' 'o,' 'e,' and 'u' sounds)*

20. Dot, Zip, and Gus *(short 'a,' 'i,' 'o,' 'e,' and 'u' sounds)*

Introduction

Blending the sounds associated with printed letters into words is an important skill in learning to read. Frequently, young children know many individual letter sounds, but need practice blending the sounds into words. *Decodable Little Books* provide brief, story-like texts for children who know most individual letter-sound correspondences for the consonants and short vowels. The books contain short words of two, three, and four letters with consistent letter sounds. They provide easy practice with decoding, and encourage children to experience a sense of accomplishment and pleasure with reading.

Not intended to be children's first experience with blending letter sounds into words, the books encourage practice with the strategy of sounding out words by using consistent consonant and short vowel sounds. In the classroom, you may use any or all of the books as a part of the curriculum for all children or as a supplement for individual or small groups of children.

The simplicity of *Decodable Little Books* allows children to read the text independently after the teacher models it. The sixth page of each book is a text-only repetition of the story that encourages children to focus on the print in order to identify words. Sometimes, beginning readers over-rely on the pictures to identify words; if they are to become fluent readers, children need to attend closely to the letters in the words.

Before introducing the *Decodable Little Books,* children should be able to orally blend sounds into words, should know printed letter–letter-sound correspondences, and have had some practice with sounding out printed words. Assessment of these prerequisite skills may be available from informal or formal screening measures performed at the end of kindergarten or beginning of first grade.

Procedures

Getting Ready for the Lessons

Present the first 10 Decodable Little Books in the same sequence that you introduce the short vowel sounds. If the children in your class are likely to be able to decode words accurately after modeling, introduce each book to a large group. If children are likely to need help with accurate decoding, introduce the books to small groups or individually so that each child's accuracy can be monitored and guided.

When you are ready to introduce a Decodable Little Book, tell children that you have a Little Book to read to them and that they will later be given a copy to read and keep at home. Plan to spend about 10 minutes with each book.

Preparing the Decodable Little Books

Each Decodable Little Book appears on four sequential pages in the *Reproducible Little Books* section of this resource. This format allows easy photocopying and assembly of the teacher's and children's copies. If possible, make one copy of each book for every child.

To prepare the copies, follow these instructions.

1. Remove the four perforated full pages that comprise one complete book, or press the book flat on a copy machine and copy the four pages.

2. Use the perforated pages or the copied pages as your master to make more copies of each Decodable Little Book. Copy and collate as many sets of the four pages as needed.

3. For each book, cut the set of four collated pages horizontally, place the set of top halves on top of the set of bottom halves to form one complete book.

4. Staple the left side of each book twice.

You may wish to make one enlarged copy of each book to use when introducing the Decodable Little Books to a group. Laminating these copies will make them sturdier. Consider adding color to the books' illustrations on the enlarged copies before laminating them. Highlighting pens work well for this.

Using the Books

Opening

- Have children sit around you. Hold the (enlarged) Decodable Little Book so that everyone can see it.

- Show children the title page of the Decodable Little Book and say, "We are going to practice our reading with this book. The title is _____." Track each letter of the title with your finger as you produce its sound in the word.

- Tell children, "You can read the words in this book by blending the sound for each letter into the words. First, I will read it to you. Then, we will read it together."

Modeling and Guiding

- Read the text slowly and clearly, tracking with your finger as you blend the individual sounds into the word. Be sure to match the letter sounds with your tracking.

- If necessary, read each page a second time, blending the individual sounds more quickly as you track the letters.

- Be sure to use a clear and animated voice. Stop after page 6.

- Give a copy of the book to each child in the group.

- Beginning with the title page, have each child read a page, in turn. In a large group, have children read in unison.

- Encourage all children to follow along by tracking with their fingers; you may need to refer to page numbers to help with this.

- If a child does not produce the correct word or blend the sounds into the correct word (even after allowing some time to self-correct), model sounding out the word for the child.

- Reread the book with children as often as necessary to assure accurate decoding.

- Be sure to respond to each child's attempts in a positive manner.

Read the words on pages 7 and 8 to children; do not expect them to decode these words. On the seventh page of each book, children can write the names of people to whom they have read the story. On the eighth and last page, children may draw pictures of the characters in the story and add words to describe their pictures.

Closing

- Conclude each presentation of a Decodable Little Book by asking several questions about the story to check comprehension.

- You might briefly discuss the story or talk about specific words in the story. Ask children to retell the story or comment on their favorite page or event in the story.

- Consider rereading a book previously presented.

- If children sometimes expect a word that differs from the actual printed word, let them know this is okay; it shows that they are reading for sense and meaning. However, remind children that they can blend each letter sound into the word to figure it out. The pictures can help, but they should focus on reading the printed words.

- As you end a session, show children where you will place the (enlarged) classroom copy of the new book so that they can read it later.

- Make sure that each child can accurately decode the text before sending children home with a Decodable Little Book.

Teacher Tips

1. Use the Decodable Little Books with kindergarten children who know the consonant and short vowel sounds and are beginning to blend letter sounds into words, as a review for all children at the beginning of first grade, or with smaller groups of children who need easy practice decoding words. Decodable Little Books are especially helpful for children who become frustrated or inattentive with more complex and extensive text.

2. Remember that the Decodable Little Books may not be appropriate for all children. Children may become bored if they find the books too hard or too easy. If children can read the texts independently and fluently without introduction by the teacher, they are probably ready for more challenging text. If children cannot read the text independently after you have modeled it and guided them through their reading, they probably need practice with one or more of the prerequisite skills.

3. Although you can make the books available to all children in the classroom (for example, during silent reading time), only provide instruction and individual copies for those needing practice with easily decodable text.

4. Children can add color to the illustrations in their personal copies of the books with crayons or markers and draw pictures on the last page of each book as in-class or at-home activities.

5. Providing children with individual copies of the books allows them to enjoy reading the books at home while building fluency with decoding short words.

6. Suggest that children keep their books in one place at home. You might encourage them to decorate special bags with handles, shoe boxes, or large envelopes for "Books I Can Read."

7. It is helpful to introduce parents to the goals and purposes of Decodable Little Books. You will find a sample letter to parents on the next page. You may want to modify the letter so that instructions to parents match your strategies for decoding words.

Decodable Little Books © Good Year Books

Sample Parent Letter

Date

Dear Parent/Guardian:

During the year, your child will be bringing home personal copies of Little Books. These books are stapled photocopies of books read in class. They are for your child to keep and read at home. Please help your child keep the Little Books in a special bag or box.

The brief text of the Little Books will help your child practice reading short words. As your child reads the books to you, answer questions he or she may have about the words. If your child gets stuck on a word, ask "What does your teacher tell you to do to figure out a word?" If your child still cannot figure out the word, point to the word and say what it is.

The most important use of the books is as enjoyable practice reading. Remember, your child is just beginning to read and will benefit from your patience and interest. You may notice that your child finds reading the words easier each time he or she reads the book.

Sincerely,

Sam the Cat

short 'a' sound

Sam the cat naps.

Sam sat.

Sam the Cat.

Sam sat.
Sam and a hat.
Sam and a mat.
Sam the cat naps.

Sam and a hat.

3

Sam the Cat

7

I read this book to:

1._____

2._____

3._____

Sam and a mat.

Sam the Cat

Picture by _____ .

Sam at Bat

short 'a' sound

Sam can tag.

Sam has a cap.

Sam at Bat

Sam has a cap.
Sam can bat.
Sam ran and ran.
Sam can tag.

3

Sam can bat.

Sam at Bat

7

I read this book to:

1._____

2._____

3._____

4

Sam ran and ran.

Sam at Bat

8

Picture by _____ **.**

Zip the Pig

short 'i' sound

5

Zip the pig sits.

2

Zip is big.

Decodable Little Books © Good Year Books

Zip the Pig

6

Zip is big.
Zip in a wig.
Zip in a bib.
Zip the pig sits.

Decodable Little Books © Good Year Books

Zip in a wig.

Zip the Pig

I read this book to:

1._____

2._____

3._____

4

Zip in a bib.

Zip the Pig

8

Picture by _____.

Zip Did It

short 'i' sound

5

Zip the pig hid.

Zip hid his wig.

Zip Did It

Zip hid his wig.
Zip hid his bib.
Zip digs.
Zip the pig hid.

3

Zip hid his bib.

Zip Did It

7

I read this book to:

1._____

2._____

3._____

Zip digs.

Zip Did It

Picture by _____ .

Dot the Fox

short 'o' sound

Dot the fox got hot.

Dot hops.

Decodable Little Books © Good Year Books

Dot the Fox

Dot hops.

Dot mops.

Dot hops and mops.

Dot the fox got hot.

Decodable Little Books © Good Year Books

Dot mops.

Dot the Fox

I read this book to:

1._____

2._____

3._____

4

Dot hops and mops.

Decodable Little Books © Good Year Books

Dot the Fox

8

Picture by _____ **.**

Decodable Little Books © Good Year Books

Dot and the Box

short 'o' sound

5

The box on Dot.

Dot on the box.

Dot and the Box

Dot on the box.
Dot hops on the box.
Dot not on the box.
The box on Dot.

Dot hops on the box.

Dot and the Box

I read this book to:

1._____

2._____

3._____

Dot not on the box.

Decodable Little Books © Good Year Books

Dot and the Box

Picture by _____.

Decodable Little Books © Good Year Books

Peg the Hen

short 'e' sound

5

Pet Peg the hen.

Peg gets fed.

Peg the Hen

Peg gets fed.
Peg's nest.
Peg's eggs.
Pet Peg the hen.

3

Peg's nest.

Peg the Hen

7

I read this book to:

1._____

2._____

3._____

4

Peg's eggs.

8

Peg the Hen

Picture by _____ **.**

4

Peg's Leg

short 'e' sound

5

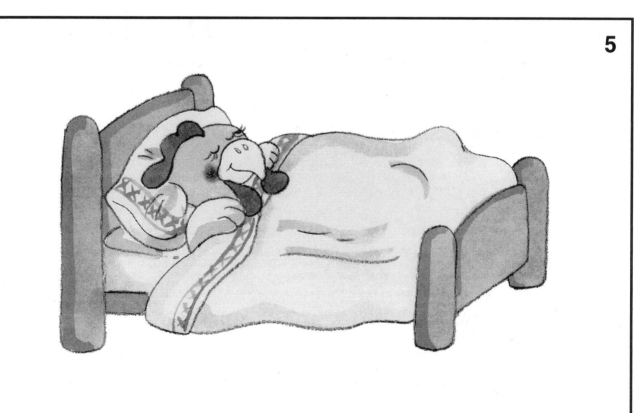

Peg in bed.

2

Peg gets wet.

Peg's Leg

6

Peg gets wet.
Peg fell.
Peg's leg is set.
Peg in bed.

Decodable Little Books © Good Year Books

Decodable Little Books © Good Year Books

Peg fell.

Peg's Leg

I read this book to:

1. _____

2. _____

3. _____

4

Peg's leg is set.

Decodable Little Books © Good Year Books

Peg's Leg

8

Picture by _____.

Decodable Little Books © Good Year Books

Gus the Bug

short 'u' sound

Rub-a-dub, Gus the bug.

Gus runs.

Gus the Bug

Gus runs.
Gus runs in mud.
Gus in the tub.
Rub-a-dub, Gus the bug.

Gus runs in mud.

Gus the Bug

I read this book to:

1._____

2._____

3._____

4

Gus in the tub.

Gus the Bug

8

Picture by _____.

Gus on the Rug

short 'u' sound

5

Fun on the rug.

Gus runs up the rug.

Gus on the Rug

Gus runs up the rug.
Gus tugs.
Gus hugs.
Fun on the rug.

3

Gus tugs.

Decodable Little Books © Good Year Books

Gus on the Rug

7

I read this book to:

1._____

2._____

3._____

Decodable Little Books © Good Year Books

4

Gus hugs.

Gus on the Rug

8

Picture by _____ .

Zip and Sam

short 'a' and 'i' sounds

Zip did win.

Zip ran. Sam ran.

Zip and Sam

Zip ran. Sam ran.
Sam ran zig-zag.
Zip can tag Sam.
Zip did win.

Sam ran zig-zag.

Zip and Sam

I read this book to:

1._____

2._____

3._____

Zip can tag Sam.

Zip and Sam

Picture by _____.

Sam and Zip

short 'a,' 'i,' and 'o' sounds

Zip hid in a box.

Sam sat on a mat.

Sam and Zip

Sam sat on a mat.
Zip sat on Sam.
Sam is mad.
Zip hid in a box.

Zip sat on Sam.

Sam and Zip

I read this book to:

1._____

2._____

3._____

4

Sam is mad.

Sam and Zip

8

Picture by _____.

Dot and Sam

short 'a,' 'i,' and 'o' sounds

5

Dot and Sam sit and sip.

Dot and Sam mop the mud.

Dot and Sam

6

Dot and Sam mop the mud.
Dot is hot. Sam is hot.
Dot can fix it.
Dot and Sam sit and sip.

Dot is hot. Sam is hot.

Dot and Sam

I read this book to:

1._____

2._____

3._____

4

Dot can fix it.

Dot and Sam

8

Picture by _____ .

Sam and Dot

short 'a,' 'i,' 'o,' and 'e' sounds

5

Yes, Dot can fit.

2

Can Sam sit on Dot's lap?

Sam and Dot

6

Can Sam sit on Dot's lap?
Yes, Sam can.
Can Dot sit on Sam's lap?
Yes, Dot can fit.

3

Yes, Sam can.

Sam and Dot

7

I read this book to:

1._____

2._____

3._____

4

Can Dot sit on Sam's lap?

Sam and Dot

8

Picture by _____.

Peg and Zip

short 'a,' 'i,' 'o,' and 'e' sounds

5

Peg can get the hat.

2

Peg has on a hat.

Peg and Zip

6

Peg has on a hat.
Zip hid Peg's hat.
It is in the bag.
Peg can get the hat.

Zip hid Peg's hat.

Peg and Zip

I read this book to:

1._____

2._____

3._____

4

It is in the bag.

Decodable Little Books © Good Year Books

Peg and Zip

8

Picture by _____.

Decodable Little Books © Good Year Books

Peg and Gus

short 'a,' 'i,' 'o,' 'e,' and 'u' sounds

Peg and Gus had fun.

2

Peg met Gus on the rug.

Peg and Gus

6

Peg met Gus on the rug.
Gus gets on top.
Peg and Gus run and run.
Peg and Gus had fun.

Gus gets on top.

Peg and Gus

I read this book to:

1._____

2._____

3._____

4

Peg and Gus run and run.

Decodable Little Books © Good Year Books

Peg and Gus

8

Picture by _____ .

Decodable Little Books © Good Year Books

Dot and Peg

short 'a,' 'i,' 'o,' 'e,' and 'u' sounds

5

Dot and Peg sit in the sun.

Dot runs up the hill.

Dot and Peg

Dot runs up the hill.
Peg runs up the hill.
Dot and Peg on the tip top.
Dot and Peg sit in the sun.

Peg runs up the hill.

Dot and Peg

I read this book to:

1._____

2._____

3._____

4

Dot and Peg on the tip top.

Dot and Peg

8

Picture by _____.

Gus and Zip

short 'a,' 'i,' 'o,' 'e,' and 'u' sounds

5

Get up, Zip! Help Gus.

2

The bag is on the bed.

Gus and Zip

6

The bag is on the bed.
Gus hid in the bag.
Zip sat on the bag.
Get up, Zip! Help Gus.

Gus hid in the bag.

Gus and Zip

I read this book to:

1._____

2._____

3._____

4

Zip sat on the bag.

Gus and Zip

8

Picture by _____.

Gus, Sam, and Peg

short 'a,' 'i,' 'o,' 'e,' and 'u' sounds

5

Gus, Sam, and Peg get hugs.

Gus sat on Sam's lap.

Gus, Sam, and Peg

**Gus sat on Sam's lap.
Peg gets on Sam's lap.
Gus and Peg can not fit.
Gus, Sam, and Peg
get hugs.**

Peg gets on Sam's lap.

Decodable Little Books © Good Year Books

Gus, Sam, and Peg

7

I read this book to:

1._____

2._____

3._____

Decodable Little Books © Good Year Books

4

Gus and Peg can not fit.

Gus, Sam, and Peg

8

Picture by _____ .

Dot, Zip, and Gus

short 'a,' 'i,' 'o,' 'e,' and 'u' sounds

Dot, Zip, and Gus hop, skip, and jump.

Gus naps on the rug.

Dot, Zip, and Gus

**Gus naps on the rug.
Dot hops and Zip skips.
Get up, Gus. Yes, get up.
Dot, Zip, and Gus hop, skip, and jump.**

3

Dot hops and Zip skips.

Dot, Zip, and Gus

7

I read this book to:

1._____

2._____

3._____

Get up, Gus. Yes, get up.

Dot, Zip, and Gus

Picture by _____.